NOW YOU CAN READ...
STORIES FROM THE
BIBLE

The stories and illustrations
in this Omnibus have been
published as separate volumes
by Pickering & Inglis.
© Brimax Rights Ltd 1983
All rights reserved
Published by Pickering & Inglis Ltd,
Basingstoke, England, 1983
Second Printing 1986
Printed in Hong Kong.
ISBN 0 7208 2332 3

CONTENTS

Noah and the Ark

Once, long long ago, an old man,
with a long beard and snowy-white
hair, was cutting tree trunks into
planks. Many people stood round him
watching to see what he was making.
The man's name was Noah. Noah was
a good man who loved God.

Noah's wife and his three sons watched him work. At last, they saw what he was making. It was a very large, strong ship.

"How can it float?" said Noah's wife. "There is no water nearby." Noah said, "This is a new kind of ship called an ark. It will have a door in the side and a roof. It will have a window and three decks."

"What is it for, husband? Why are you making the ark?" said Noah's wife.

"God has told me to make the ark," said Noah. "He will send rain which will cover the land. Every living thing will die because His people have been wicked. We must go inside the ark with our sons and their children. We must take with us two of every kind of animal. The ark will float on the water and all inside it will be safe."

"We will need food for everyone
and food for the animals," said
Noah's wife. So, Noah and his wife
and three sons began to make plans
for their stay in the ark.

Sacks of grain and bags of salt were put on the deck of the ark. Barrels of fresh water for drinking were filled. Hay and straw for the animals were laid inside the ark.

They found the animals and took
them onto the ark. There was
every kind of animal there,
elephants, lions and camels.

There were dogs, cats, birds,
snakes and even mice and worms.

Noah told everyone to hurry, for
he could see the rain coming. He
pushed two donkeys from behind.
"Come along, you slow donkeys, get
on board if you do not want to
get your feet wet!"

When everyone and everything was inside, Noah closed the door. Soon, great black clouds filled the sky and rain began to fall.

Day after day it rained, until all the land was covered with water. The rain fell for forty days and forty nights. The ark was lifted. It floated high in the water.

The water covered the land for many, many days. Inside the ark, everyone was becoming tired, for it was noisy and there was little food left.

A dog growled, as if to say, "My straw is not soft. I cannot sleep."

On the other side of the ark, the giraffes were very unhappy. The roof was so low that they had to bend their heads. They had very stiff necks.

At last, the rain stopped, and the
waters went down. The ark came to
rest upon a mountain. Noah looked
out to see how he could tell
when it would be safe to leave
the ark.

He went to where the birds rested
and spoke to the big, black raven.
"Go out, raven
and fly over the
land. If you can
find a tree in
which to rest,
then stay there.
If you cannot find
a tree, then fly
back to the ark."
The raven was away
all day. It did
not come back.
"I will wait a
little longer,"
said Noah.

23

A week later, Noah sent out a dove.

The little dove came back to the ark, for she knew there was food there.
"I will wait a little longer," said Noah. "I think things will be better soon."

He waited seven days and let the
dove out again.
When night came, Noah saw the dove
coming back. It held in its beak
a green olive leaf.

"The leaves have grown again on
the trees," cried Noah. "Now we
can leave the ark."

The door was opened. Noah and his family came out of the ark.

The animals and birds were glad to be free again on dry land. God had spared Noah, and all his family from the flood. They gave thanks to God.

"Look! Look up there in the sky,"
cried Noah's wife. Right across the
sky was a lovely rainbow. This was
God's promise that He would never
again flood the world.
Sometimes, when it has been raining,
if you look up into the sky, you
too, can see a rainbow.

All these appear in the pages of
the story. Can you find them?

Noah

Noah's wife

ark

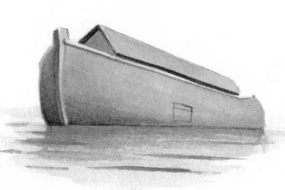

two donkeys

rainbow

dove

mountain

rain

Now tell the story in your own words.

Moses in the
Bulrushes

Long ago, in a country called Egypt,
there lived a girl named Miriam.
She was twelve years old. Her
hair was long and dark, and her
face was gentle. She had a brother
called Aaron. He was a good boy
and helped his father with the
work. Their mother had another
child, a little boy. He was a
happy baby. He laughed and smiled
at them from his cradle.

They all lived in a small, dark
house, near a great river called
the Nile. It was warm during the
day but cold at night, in that
little house.

Not far away stood a great white
palace. It was where the king
lived. He was the ruler of Egypt
and he was a proud and cruel man.
He wanted to be king of Egypt for
as long as he lived. He did not
want anyone else to take his place.

Miriam came from a good family and her friends were good people, but the king did not like them. He had a very cruel plan. He said that every baby boy had to be killed.

Outside the big white palace marched the soldiers who guarded the king. They were hard and cruel like the king.

When they heard what the king wanted, they said they would help him. They would go to the houses and take away every baby boy. They would throw them into the river.

Miriam said, "What shall we do, mother? I do not want the soldiers to find my little brother and take him away."

"Do not be afraid, Miriam," said her mother. "I have a plan, wait and see."

As the baby was three months old, he was a strong child and his crying was very loud. His mother was worried that one of the king's cruel soldiers would hear him.

She picked some bulrushes from behind the house.

She made a basket, shaped like a cradle. On the outside, she spread black tar, so that the water could not get in. Inside, she put a lovely soft cloth.

39

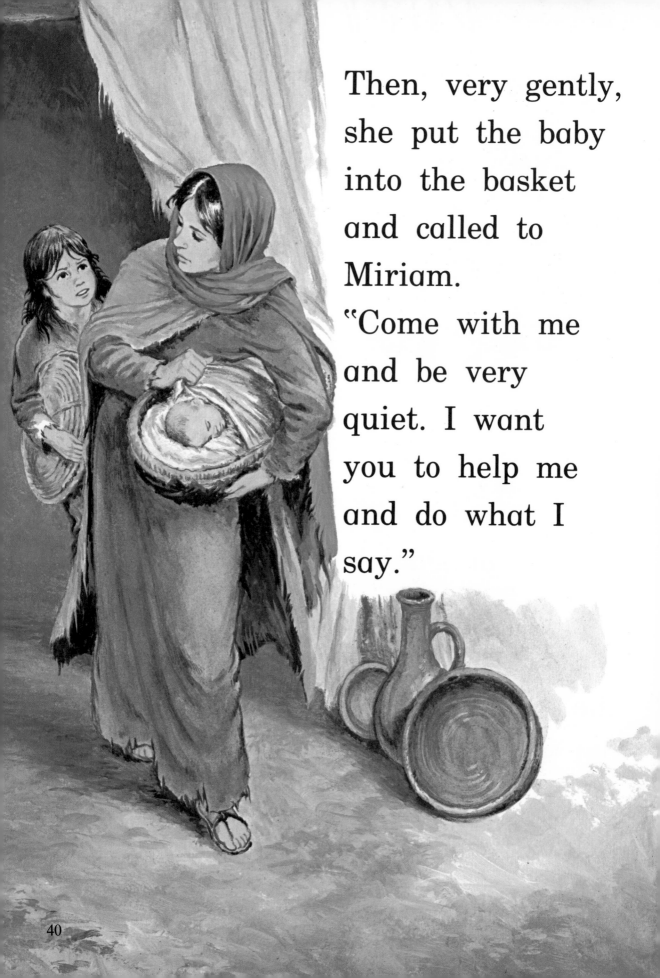

Then, very gently, she put the baby into the basket and called to Miriam. "Come with me and be very quiet. I want you to help me and do what I say."

They crept down to the side of the river and looked for a good place to put the basket. It could not go where the water ran or it would float away.

They hid the basket in a clump of bulrushes and Miriam sat down behind it.

"You must stay here, Miriam," said
her mother. "Watch the basket.
This is just the place where the
king's daughter comes to swim. She
will find your little brother here.
She will take him to the palace.
If she does, then he will be safe."

Miriam sat very still behind the bulrushes. She was afraid. Before long, she heard voices and girls laughing. The princess was walking along the path. A slave held a sun-shade over her.

Miriam held her breath. Her little
brother had begun to cry, for he
was hungry by that time.

"What's that?" called the princess.
"A basket is hidden there. Go and
bring it to me."

One of the
servant girls
paddled out
into the
water.

She lifted up
the basket and
took it back to
the princess.
She lifted the
lid. There was
the poor baby,
crying and
kicking his
legs.

45

The princess didn't know much about babies, but she picked him up and cuddled him. Soon he was quiet.

"What a lovely child!" she cried.
"I would like to keep him."

Miriam stood up
and walked
forward.
"Do you need a
nurse for your
baby? I know
someone who
would be pleased
to help you," she
said.
"Yes," said the
princess. "I do
need a nurse.
Will you bring
her to me?"

Miriam ran home and told her mother what had happened. They hurried back to where the princess was waiting.

"You may take him away and look after him," said the princess to Miriam's mother. "I shall see that you are paid. When he is older you must bring him back to me."

So Miriam, the
baby and their
mother went back
to the dark,
little house.
They lived
there safely.
When the baby
was older, his
mother took
him to the
palace. The
princess loved
the little boy
and she called
him Moses.

All these appear in the pages of the story. Can you find them?

mother

Miriam

king

baby

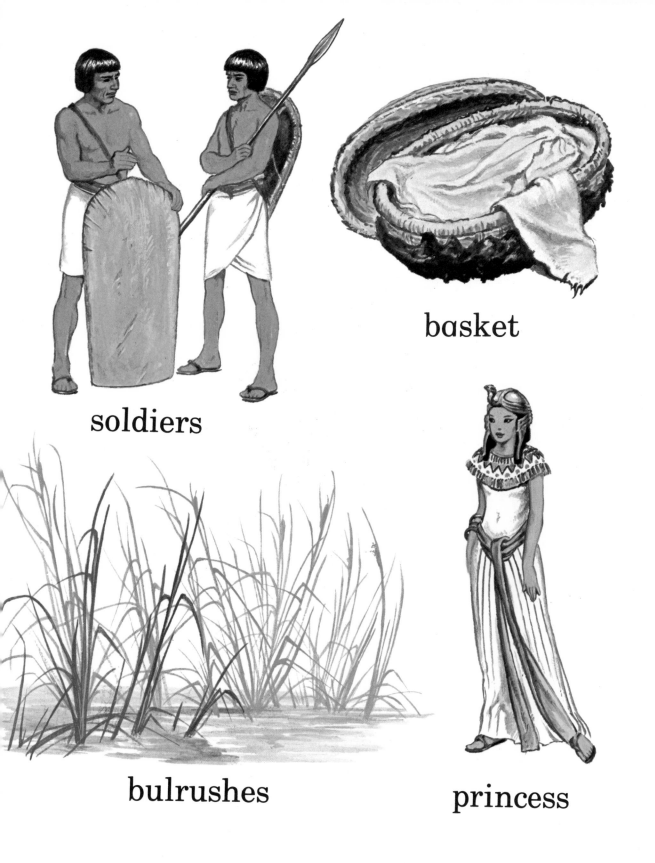

soldiers

basket

bulrushes

princess

Now tell the story in your own words.

Moses the Leader

A boy called Moses lived in a great palace. It was the home of the king of Egypt. The king's daughter had looked after Moses since he was a baby. She had found Moses lying in a cradle. It was hidden in the bulrushes near the river. His mother had hidden him there. She was afraid of the cruel king. The king's name was Pharaoh.

As she sat by a pool, the princess told Moses about his people. Many years ago, she said, Moses' people had to come to Egypt to look for food. The cruel king had made them slaves. He made them work very hard.

When Moses became older, he went
out to watch the slaves. They dug
clay to make bricks. They chopped
straw to mix with water. It held
the clay together. The wet bricks
were put to dry in the hot sun.
Pharaoh made the slaves build great
cities. If they stopped to rest,
his cruel soldiers hit them with
whips. Moses was sad and angry.
His people were not free. They
were not happy.

Moses left the palace. He went across the desert into another land. Many years passed. Moses became a shepherd. One day, as he was looking after his sheep on the hillside, God sent him a sign. Moses saw a bush in front of him. It burst into flames but the flames did not burn the bush.

A voice called to Moses. It came from the middle of the bush.

"Moses, take off your shoes and come near. This is holy ground." It was the voice of God.

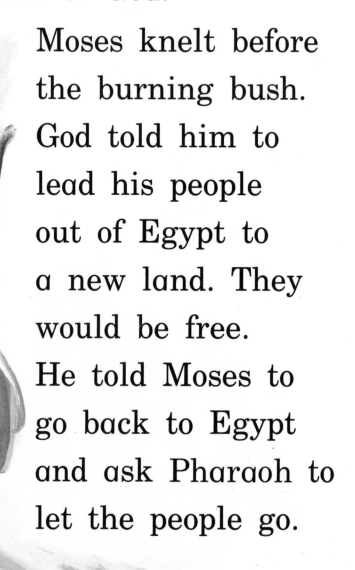

Moses knelt before the burning bush. God told him to lead his people out of Egypt to a new land. They would be free. He told Moses to go back to Egypt and ask Pharaoh to let the people go.

Moses went back to Egypt. He found his brother Aaron. They called the slaves together to tell them what God had said.

The people bowed their heads and gave thanks to God.

Moses and Aaron went to the palace. They came before the king to tell him of God's words.

Pharaoh became very angry.

"Why should I listen to your God? I need slaves to work for me. I will never let them go!"

Pharaoh told his soldiers to beat
the slaves. He knew they would
work harder. So God punished
Pharaoh in many ways. Then the
king's people became afraid. They
begged Pharaoh to let the slaves
go. Pharaoh called Moses.

"Go," he said. "Take your children
and your animals. Go from this
land."

Moses helped his people make ready to leave. They tied things in bundles. Cattle and sheep were herded together. Their cooking pots and water jars were slung across oxen. They then made their way on foot, out of the land of Egypt. They had been slaves for more than four hundred years.

Moses led his people across the desert. There was little water or food. The children cried. They were hot and tired. The people were afraid.

"Do not be afraid," said Moses. "God will show us the way."

God did not forget them. By day, He sent a pillar of cloud in front of them. It showed them the way to go.

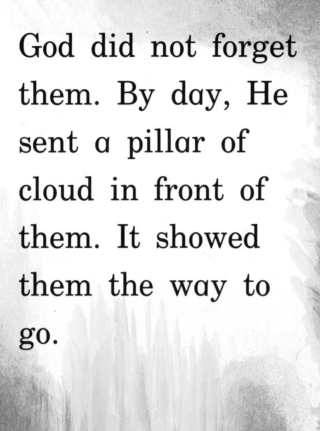

At night, a pillar of fire glowed in the dark, so that they could see.

In Egypt, people
were angry.
Without the slaves,
there was no one
to do the work.
Pharaoh sent six
hundred soldiers
to bring back
the slaves.

Moses and his people came to the
Red Sea. They could not cross the
sea. They said to Moses, "Why
have you led us here to die?"

"God will help us," said Moses.
God put a pillar of cloud between
them and Pharaoh's army. The
soldiers could not see them.

Then God said to Moses, "Lift your staff over the sea. The sea will part and leave a path in the middle. Your people can cross to the other side."

Moses did as he was told. There came a mighty wind. The sea rolled back.

Moses and his people crossed to
the other side. They saw Pharaoh's
men follow. What could they do?
They were lost.

God told Moses to stretch his hand over the sea. When he did so, the waves crashed like thunder. The waters of the sea came together. The sea covered the soldiers. Not one was left.

Moses and his people fell onto
their knees to thank God. God had
saved them. They were free. At
last they were going to the land
God had given them.

All these appear in the pages of the story. Can you find them?

Moses

Princess

Pharaoh

slaves

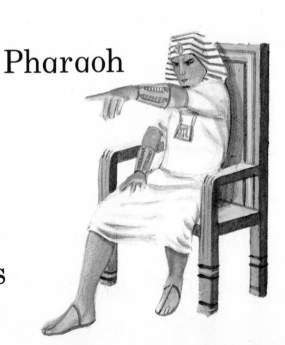

bush

soldiers

pillar of cloud

waves

Now tell the story in your own words.

Samuel

One day, in a place called Shiloh,
the people took their children to
pray in God's house. It was called
the Temple.

The Temple was a
holy place. Inside
was an altar of
wood and a shining
lamp. Behind the
altar, a tent hid
the Ark of God.
Inside, lay
the holy laws
God had given
to the people.

When the people
came out of the
Temple, they had
a great feast.

The children sang and had a happy
time.

One woman, whose name was Hannah,
sat alone. She had no children.
She wished that she could have just
one child. Year after year she
waited. No child was born. Hannah
was very sad.

She left the feast
and walked back to
the Temple. At
the door, sat the
old priest Eli.
Hannah walked past
him and knelt down.

She prayed to God.
She asked Him to
send her a baby.
"If I have a
son," she said, "I
will give him back
to you. He will
do your work."

Eli went up to her and said,
"What is the matter?"
She told him and he said,
"Go in peace. May God give you
what you want."
Hannah felt happy as she went back
to the feast.
Very soon, God gave Hannah a little
son. She called him Samuel.

She did not forget her promise to
God. When Samuel was five years
old, she made him a little coat.
She took him with her to the
Temple.
She went to Eli
and said,
"I am the woman
who asked God for
a son. God has
heard my prayer.
This is the boy
He sent me. Now
I am giving him
back to God as
I promised."

Samuel was a good boy. Eli looked after him as if he were his own.

Every year, his mother went to see him. She took him a new coat.

Samuel helped Eli each day in the Temple.

Eli had two sons.
They did not help
him. They made
fun of holy things
and spent their
time in Shiloh.
Eli knew that his
sons did wicked
things, but he
said nothing.

Eli was very old
and nearly blind.
Samuel led Eli
everywhere.

Samuel slept in a corner of the Temple, near the lamp of gold. He had to see that the lamp was always kept burning. Samuel kept the oil ready.

One night, he woke up. He heard
a voice calling "Samuel, Samuel."
He thought it was
Eli calling him.
He ran through the
Temple to where
Eli lay.
"I did not call
you," Eli said.
"Go back to sleep."

Again the voice called and once again, Samuel ran to Eli.
"I did not call you," said Eli.

When the voice called a third time,
Eli knew that it was God who
spoke to the boy. He said,
"If you hear the voice again, you
must say, 'Speak, Lord, I can hear
you'."

Samuel did as Eli told him. He was not afraid. He waited. All was still in the Temple. The lamp glowed softly. God spoke to Samuel and said, "The sons of Eli are very wicked. Eli knows this. I shall punish Eli and his sons. You must tell Eli what I have said."

Samuel was sad. He loved Eli. He did not want to tell him what God had said.

Samuel could not sleep. He walked outside the Temple until the morning.

Then, as Eli sat under a great
tree outside the Temple, Samuel told
him God's words. Eli put his hands
over his face.
"God will do what is right," he
said at last.

At night in the Temple, God spoke many times to Samuel. People came from far away to hear Samuel. He told the people what God wanted them to do.

The years went by and war broke out. The people sent a message to the Temple. They wanted the Ark. They thought that God would help them if they carried it. Eli's wicked sons took the Ark from the Temple.

The Ark was carried into battle.

The Ark was taken by the enemy.
Eli's sons were killed in the
battle.

A man who had been in the fighting came to tell Eli about the battle. He found Eli sitting outside the Temple.

When Eli heard that the Ark of God had been taken, he died. The old man's heart was broken.

Samuel prayed to God to help the people. He told them to serve God. The people listened to Samuel for he spoke the word of God.

All these appear in the pages of the story. Can you find them?

Temple

Ark

lamp

children

Hannah

Eli

sons

Samuel

Now tell the story in your own words.

David and Goliath

David was a shepherd boy. He looked after his father's sheep. He had to see that no one came to steal the sheep. If a wild animal came close, he had to chase it away. David had seven brothers. He was the youngest in the family.

One day, as he was
playing his harp in
the field, he saw
someone coming. He
jumped up and ran
to meet him. It
was one of his
father's servants.

The servant said, "Leave the sheep, David. Come back to your father's house. Someone wants to see you. I will look after the sheep while you are gone."

David ran quickly to the house.

His face was red as he ran inside.

His father was standing next to
another man, and said to David,
"This man is called Samuel. He
wants to meet you. He has a
special job for you to do."

Samuel knew that when David grew up, he would be the king of the country. He was still a boy, but Samuel wanted to make sure that he was the right person and would make a good king.

Samuel talked to David and then he went away.

At that time, the king of the country was a man called Saul. He was not a very good king. Sometimes he felt unhappy and would not speak to anyone. "Perhaps if someone played some cheerful music for King Saul, it would make him feel happy," said one of the servants.

David could play lovely music on the harp. He was asked to go to the palace and play for King Saul. He played some happy music and sang songs and soon the King was more cheerful.

"I want you to stay here at the palace," said King Saul. "Send a message to your father to tell him where you are."

David liked being at the palace. He talked to the King about his home and the lambs in the fields. Soon after David had gone to the palace, war broke out. King Saul had to get his army ready.

Three of David's brothers were in the army, so he had to go back to his father.

One day, David took some new bread to his brothers. He liked to go and see the fighting.

He was talking to his brothers when a great shout was heard. A huge man, like a giant, was walking towards them.

"Who will fight with me?" he roared. "If he wins, then you have won this battle, but if I win, then you will all be in our power."

"Who is going to fight him?" asked
David.

"No one dares to fight Goliath,"
said one of the soldiers. "No one
could stand up to a man like that."
David knew at once what he should
do. He went to King Saul.

"I will fight Goliath," he said.
"You!" cried King Saul. "You are only a child. Goliath is a real fighter. You cannot fight him."
"I may be small," said David, "but with God's help I have killed bears and lions when they came to steal my father's sheep. Please, let me try."

King Saul took off the suit of
armour which he was wearing and put
it on David. It was much too big.
He tripped over.

"I cannot wear this," said David.
"It is too heavy and too big.
Please take it off." The armour
was taken off and David felt much
better.

He took his sling
and went to a
little stream
nearby. He chose
five smooth stones
and put them in
a bag. Then he
walked towards the
giant.

111

Goliath could not believe his eyes. A little boy was coming to fight him! He put down his great head and charged. David took one of the stones out of his bag and put it in his sling.

He spun the sling around his head, faster and faster and let it go.

The stone flew through the air and hit Goliath right in the middle of his forehead. He crashed to the ground like a fallen tree.

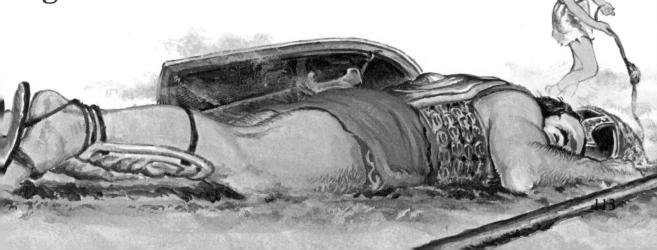

David ran up to him and took the sword from Goliath's side. With one blow he cut off Goliath's head. All the soldiers cheered and shouted. The enemy turned and ran away.

King Saul spoke to David. "You shall stay with us now. You will not return to your father's house. My son, Jonathan, will be a good friend to you."

Jonathan was very kind to David and they became like brothers.

All these appear in the pages of
the story. Can you find them?

David

sheep

Samuel

King Saul

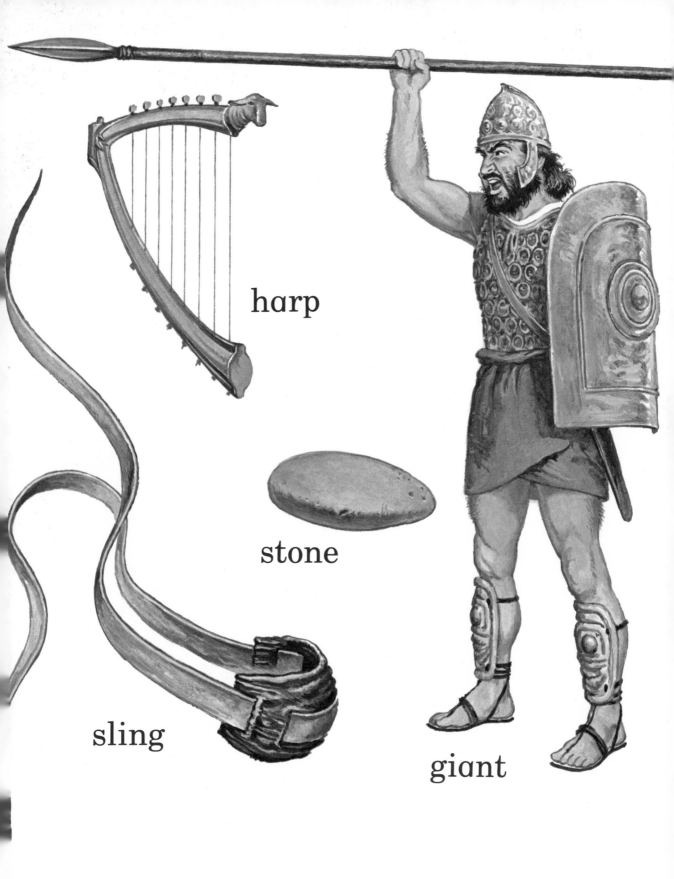

harp

stone

sling

giant

Now tell the story in your own words.

David and Jonathan

David was a young shepherd boy.
His father had eight sons and he
was the youngest. The older boys
became soldiers in the king's army.
David was left at home to look
after the sheep.

One day, a stranger named Samuel came to David's home. He told David that God had chosen David to be a king when he was older. David was surprised, but he did not say anything.

Some time later, David was taken to
see the king of the country who
was King Saul. David was very good
at playing the harp. King Saul
liked to listen to him play. He
asked David to stay at the palace
with him.

David was a gentle boy and a brave one too. Once, a great giant named Goliath, came with his army against King Saul. No one dared to face the giant, but with God's help, David stood up to him. He killed Goliath with a stone thrown from his sling. King Saul made David a leader in his army.

When the army came home after the battle, people came out of their houses. They danced and sang in the streets. Everyone was happy. The people loved David. Everyone said how brave he had been. King Saul was very angry. He was afraid the people would make David king in his place.

From that time, whenever King Saul saw David, he became angry.

One day, the King threw a spear at David to pin him to the wall. David ran from the room. David became very unhappy living at the palace. He became afraid of King Saul.

Jonathan, the King's son, was kind. He was a good friend to David. They made a promise to each other that, what-ever happened, they would always be friends.

"I can see you are not happy here," said Jonathan. "You must leave the palace. Take my armour, my sword and my bow, in case you need them."

David did not go. He did not think that he was in real danger.

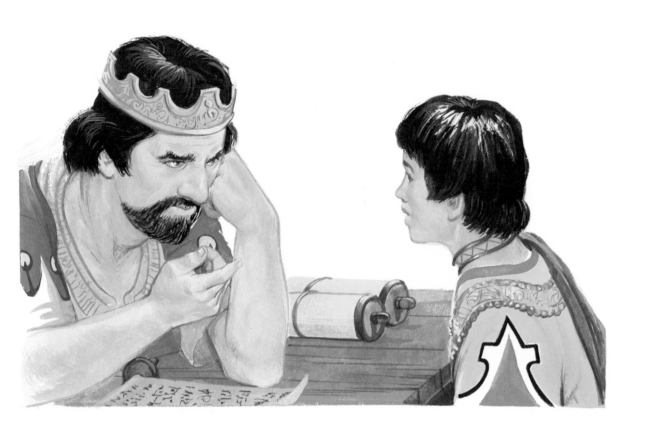

King Saul came to hate David. He told Jonathan to kill him. But Jonathan loved David and so he made a plan.

"In a field not far from here, there is a great stone," said Jonathan. "Go and hide behind it. In three days, I will come with my servant and shoot three arrows by its side. If I say to my servant, 'Go and find the arrows, they are beside the great stone,' then you will know that all is well. But, if I say, 'Find the arrows, they are ahead of you,' then you will know that there is great danger. You must go away."

So David hid behind the great
stone. Jonathan went to King Saul.
He begged him not to kill David.
King Saul did not listen. He
became very angry. He threw his
sword at Jonathan, but it missed
him.

Jonathan ran from the palace, calling his servant. He went to the field near the great stone. Soon his arrows flew through the air.

"Find the arrows,"
called Jonathan.
"They are ahead
of you!"

David heard and he was very sad.
The servant found the arrows.
Jonathan sent him home.

Then David came out of his hiding place. He put his arms round Jonathan.

"My father is so angry. I am sure he plans to kill you. You must go away," said Jonathan. "Hide far away from here. You must remember our promise. We shall always be friends."

David ran away. He found a cave
near the desert, where he lived
for a long time.

Other men who were afraid of King Saul joined David. When he was older, he became their leader.

One day, someone
asked to see
David.

It was Jonathan. A long time had
passed. Jonathan hardly knew him.
They threw their arms round each
other.

"You need not be afraid," said Jonathan. "My father will never find you. One day, you will be king and I shall serve you. Until then, we must part."

Jonathan went back to join his father's army.

Some years later, David heard that there had been a great battle. One day, a soldier from King Saul's camp came to David. His clothes were torn. David could see that he had been in the fighting. He told David that King Saul and Jonathan were dead. He brought the King's crown with him. He gave it to David.

David wept. He was very, very sad. God had made him a king, but David had lost his best and dearest friend.

All these appear in the pages of the story. Can you find them?

Jonathan

Goliath

David

King Saul

arrows

the great stone

crown

cave

Now tell the story in your own
words.

The Birth of Jesus

Long ago, in a small town called Nazareth, there lived a girl named Mary. At that time, many men had forgotten about God. He decided to send a little child to live and grow up among the people. This little child would teach them about God.

God knew that Mary loved Him, so He chose her to be the mother of His child. He sent an angel called Gabriel to tell Mary about the baby. Mary was alone in her house when she saw the angel standing beside her. She was afraid and hid her eyes.

The angel looked kindly at Mary and said, "Do not be afraid, Mary. God has sent me to tell you good news. Soon you will have a baby. It will be a boy and his name will be Jesus. He will be a holy child, for he will be the Son of God."

In the same town, a carpenter called
Joseph lived. He wanted to take
care of Mary and the baby, because
he loved her. Joseph took Mary
to be his wife.

The king of the land wanted all the people to be counted, so Mary and Joseph had to go back to the place where they were born.

It was a long way to go, so they had a little donkey for Mary to ride while Joseph walked by her side. At last, they came to an inn.

They were very tired
and needed a rest.
Joseph knocked at
the door. The door
opened and the
inn-keeper said,
"What do you
want?"
"Have you a bed
for the night,
please?" asked
Joseph. "My wife
is very tired, for
we have come a
long way."

"I am very sorry," said the inn-keeper, shaking his head. "There is no room for you here. If you would like to stay in the stable with the animals, you are welcome to rest there. It is warm and dry."

"Thank you," said Joseph. "That will do very well."

They followed the inn-keeper to the
stable, and there in the night, the
baby Jesus was born.

There was nothing for the baby to wear. Mary wrapped him in strips of cloth. There was nowhere for the baby to sleep. Joseph made him a little bed in the place where food for the cows and donkeys was kept. It was called a manger. He put warm, dry straw in it and Mary laid the baby there to sleep.

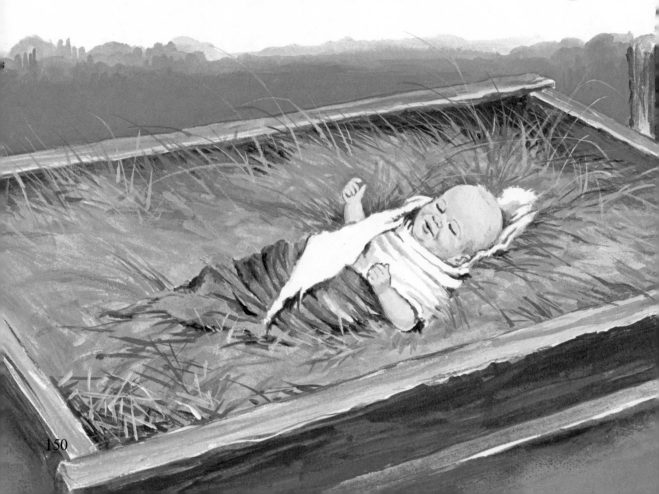

Outside, the night was dark and cold. In the fields close to the town, some shepherds were looking after their sheep. They sat close to the fire, warming their hands and talking to each other.

Suddenly, a great light shone in the sky and an angel stood in front of them.

They were all afraid but the angel said,

"Do not be afraid, for I have come to tell you good news. Tonight, the Lord Jesus has been born. Go to him. Follow the bright star in the sky and it will lead you to the stable where he lies."

Then the sky was filled with angels who sang,

"Glory to God in Heaven
Peace on Earth
And Joy to all Men"

At once the shepherds set off,
following a bright star in the sky
which led them to the place where
Jesus lay. With them they took
their sheep in case a wolf should
attack them.

The shepherds knocked at the stable door and Joseph let them in.

They knelt down beside the baby because they knew he was very special.

Mary did not know why anyone should come to see her baby, but she said nothing.

Then the shepherds left the stable and went into the town to let everyone know about Jesus.

Three wise men from the East had been keeping watch on the stars in the sky. They knew that a great king was to be born. They were waiting for a sign to show where to find him.

At last, a bright star showed them the way.

They rode across many lands following
the star. They thought they would
find him in a palace, but the star
led them to a poor stable. They
left their camels outside and going
in, found Jesus lying in a manger.

At once they knew that he was the one they had been seeking.

Each wise man had brought a present for Jesus which was laid down beside him.

When they had gone, Mary thought
again for a long time. Why had
the shepherds and the wise men
come so far to see her baby?
Then she picked up
Jesus and held him
close to her,
thinking about
what the angel
had said.

All these appear in the pages of the story. Can you find them?

Mary

angel

Joseph

donkey

inn-keeper

Jesus

manger

star

shepherds

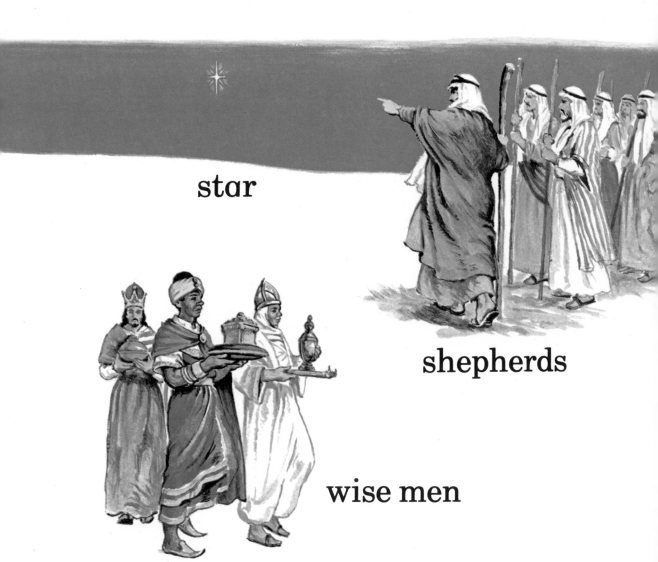

wise men

Now tell the story in your own words.

The Childhood
of Jesus

On a cold, dark night, many years ago, a little baby boy was born. His mother called him Jesus. The baby's mother was called Mary and her husband was Joseph. Shepherds from nearby and wise men from far lands went to see Jesus because he was a special baby.

The king of the country, which was called Judea, was King Herod. He did not go to see the baby. He was angry when he heard that Jesus was born. It was said that Jesus was to be a king when he grew up. King Herod did not want another king in his country. He had a very cruel plan. All the little children under two years old would be killed. In that way, he could be sure that Jesus would not live.

One night, Joseph had a dream. In
the dream he saw King Herod and
heard his plan. Joseph knew that
the baby Jesus was in great danger.
He heard a kind voice say to him,
"Take Mary and the child away from
this place. Go to Egypt and stay
there until it is safe."

Joseph woke up.
He put all they
needed into a bag
and he untied a
donkey.

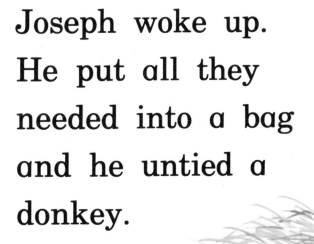

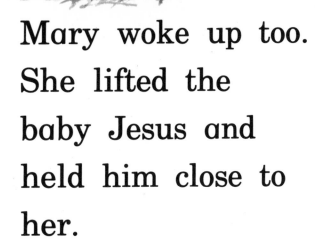

Mary woke up too.
She lifted the
baby Jesus and
held him close to
her.

Then she climbed on to the donkey
and Joseph led them out of the
town.

They walked many miles until they
reached Egypt. There they lived
for a short time.

One day, Joseph heard that King Herod had died. His son had become king in his place. Joseph decided to return to his own land, but to keep away from the big towns. They made their way back to the little town of Nazareth.

There, they unpacked and tried to make their home comfortable. Rugs were laid on the floor.

Mary washed the cooking pots and ground some corn to make bread. Joseph was a carpenter. He began to make wooden tables and yokes for oxen so that he could earn a living.

In this poor, little home, Jesus
grew from a baby to a boy.
When he was about
six years old, he
went to school.

He learned to read and he was told stories about Moses and David. He helped Joseph to put away the tools at the end of the day.

He asked Mary and Joseph many questions. Sometimes, Mary and Joseph were surprised that Jesus knew so much.

Every year, Mary and Joseph went
with the other village people to
the big city of Jerusalem. They
joined together in a special meal.
They sang songs and said prayers
to God.

When the boys were twelve years old, they could go with their parents. Jesus was glad when he could go too.

It was a long way to Jerusalem, but at last they reached the city and made camps.

In Jerusalem, there was a large
building called the Temple. Inside
the Temple sat many clever teachers
who read books to the people about
God.

Jesus listened and talked to them for
long time. They were surprised at
what he knew.

Jesus forgot about
Mary and Joseph.
He slept curled
up in a corner
near the walls
of the Temple
and early the
next morning,
he went inside
again.

The other people were packing up
and starting back home.

All day long they walked, stopping
at night to eat and rest.

Mary saw that Jesus was not with them. She ran looking for Jesus, but she could not find him. She was very worried in case he had been hurt.

Joseph and Mary walked all the way back to Jerusalem looking for Jesus.

"Let us go and look in the Temple," said Joseph. "That was the last place where he was seen."

They found Jesus with the teachers, talking and listening.

"We have been so worried about you," said Mary. "Why did you stay behind when we left yesterday?" Jesus said, "I thought you would know that I was in God's house and that I have His work to do."

Mary and Joseph did not know what Jesus meant, but they often thought about his words.

All these appear in the pages of the story. Can you find them?

Jesus

Mary

King Herod

Joseph

dream

Jerusalem

Temple

teachers

Now tell the story in your own words.

Stories Jesus Told

Jesus lived with his family in a village called Nazareth. Mary, his mother, looked after the house. Joseph was a carpenter. He made things out of wood. He worked hard. Jesus helped Joseph each day. People came from far and near to hear Jesus speak about God. He told them stories to show them the way God wanted them to live.

One day, Jesus stood on the hillside. The people sat around Him. He spoke to them about a rich man who had two sons. The two boys worked with their father on a farm.

The elder son
helped his father
plant the seeds.
He helped to look
after the pigs
and the sheep.

The younger son
did not like work.
He lay in the
sun and left the
others to do all
the hard work.

One day, the younger son said to his father, "I do not want to stay here. I want to be with my friends. Give me my share of the farm. I do not want to wait until I am old."

His father was very sad. He did not want to see his son go away. At last he gave him some money. He waved to his son as he went away across the fields. He did not know if he would ever see him again.

At first, the boy
was very happy.
He bought himself
fine clothes. He
went out with his
friends, eating
and drinking.

Soon, he had
spent all his
money. His
friends went
away and left
him. He was
very lonely.

He went to many places looking for work. He was very hungry. A farmer gave him the job of looking after his pigs.

He was so hungry that he even wanted the food that was given to the pigs.

One day, as he sat on the hot
dusty ground, watching the pigs, he
said, "I will go home to my father.
I am very sorry for what I have
done. My father looks after his
servants better than this. Maybe
he will let me be his servant."

Now his father
was a very kind
man. Every day
he went to the
top of the hill
to see if his
son was coming
home.
One day, very
far away he
saw someone
coming. He
was sure it
was his son.

He ran to the servants, saying "Make a feast for everyone. At last my son has come home. Bring out my best cloak for him to wear."

The elder son had been hard at work. He heard his father's words. He was very upset. It did not seem fair. He had stayed at home to help on the farm. He had worked very hard. His brother had wasted his time and his money. Now his father was pleased to see his brother. He was making a feast for his lazy son!

The father saw that his son was angry. He put his arms around him. He said to him, "Come, let us all be happy together. I thought your brother had gone for good. He was lost and now he is found."

Jesus wanted to teach the people that God loves everyone – no matter what she or he may have done.

Another story Jesus told is called
The Good Samaritan.

One day, a trader was on his way
from one town to another. It was
a long, hard journey. Many people
had been attacked by robbers. The
robbers hid in the caves dug out
of the rocky hillside.

As the man went on his way,
robbers came from behind some rocks.
They hit him with their sticks.

The man fell to the ground. He
was hurt and bleeding. They took
all his money and his donkey.
They ran away.

Soon a priest came by, on his way to the Temple. "Is that man dead?" he asked. "If I stop, I shall not be able to go to the Temple."

So he did not stop. He went by on the other side of the road.

After a while, another man came by, on his donkey. He was going to sing in the Temple. He saw the poor man lying there in the hot sun. He too passed by. He looked the other way.

A little later, a man from the land called Samaria came by.

He stopped when he saw the man lying on the ground. He saw that the man was badly hurt.
The Samaritan washed the man's cuts and put a clean cloth over them.
He helped the man on to his donkey.

Slowly they went on their way until they came to an inn.

The Samaritan spoke to the inn-keeper. He said, "Please look after this man. He has been beaten. All his goods have been stolen. Here is some money to pay you. I will come this way again. If you need more money, I will give it to you then."

The Samaritan went on his way.

Jesus said to the people, "Which man would you have to be your friend?" They said, "The Samaritan because he helped the man who was hurt." "Yes," said Jesus. "Now you must go and always help those who cannot help themselves."

Jesus told many more stories. The stories Jesus told are called parables.

All these appear in the pages of
the story. Can you find them?

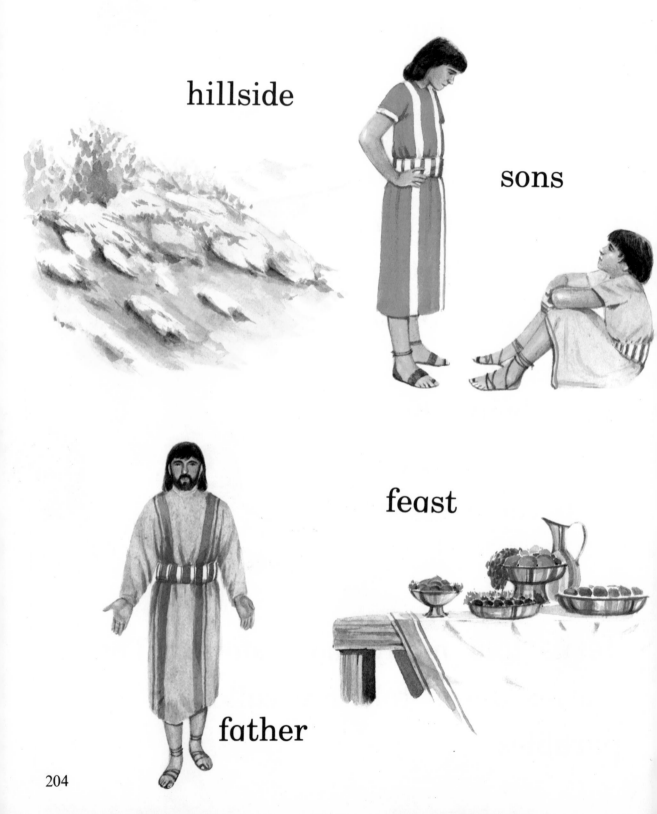

hillside

sons

feast

father

trader

robbers

Samaritan

priest

Now tell the story in your own words.